D0966029

Making Money Grow

Kathleen E. Bradley

Consultants

Timothy Rasinski, Ph.D.
Kent State University

Lori Oczkus
Literacy Consultant

Rich Levitt,
Certified Public Accountant

Based on writing from
TIME For Kids. *TIME For Kids* and the *TIME For Kids* logo are registered trademarks of
TIME Inc. Used under license.

Publishing Credits

Dona Herweck Rice, *Editor-in-Chief*
Lee Aucoin, *Creative Director*
Jamey Acosta, *Senior Editor*
Lexa Hoang, *Designer*
Stephanie Reid, *Photo Editor*
Shelly Buchanan, *Contributing Author*
Rachelle Cracchiolo, *M.S.Ed., Publisher*

Image Credits: pp.19 (bottom), 55 (top)
Associated Press; p.18 Earl Wilson/The New York
Times/Redux; p.41 (left) Fabian Fernandez-Han;
pp.23, 49 Getty Images; pp.12 (left), 39, 51
iStockphoto; p.41 (right) Javier Fernandez-Han;
pp.5, 55 (bottom), 20 PhotoResearchers Inc.; p.25
(middle) ABACAUSA.COM/Newscom; pp.22, 25
(bottom) Newscom; p.53 (bottom) REUTERS/
Newscom; p.44 TORONTO STAR/Newscom; p.64
Photography by Greg Figge; pp.10–11, 14–15,
45, 51 (illustrations) Timothy J. Bradley; All other
images from Shutterstock.

Teacher Created Materials

5301 Oceanus Drive
Huntington Beach, CA 92649-1030
http://www.tcmpub.com
ISBN 978-1-4333-4908-9
© 2013 Teacher Created Materials, Inc.

Table of Contents

Working with Others

Growing up has its advantages. At some point, you will create a home of your own. You'll cook and eat the food you love most, purchase some of the items you have always wanted, and do many of the fun activities you've dreamed of doing. You will become **self-reliant**. When you work, you get paid for your **labor**, and with a regular income, you can plan your future. There are lots of ways to make money. But it won't matter how much money you make if you don't know how to make your money grow.

✦ Why is it important to
earn money?

✦ What are some ways
you can earn money?

✦ How can you make the
money you have grow?

Allowance

Some children are given an **allowance** from their parents. An allowance is a payment of a set amount. Often, it depends on the child being responsible for **chores** around the house. An allowance gives kids an opportunity to learn how to manage money. Pay attention to where and when you spend your allowance, and keep track of what you save to manage your money wisely!

Piggy Banks

Pig-shaped banks have been around for a long time. Hundreds of years ago in England, people kept their coins in a small jar. It was made of a kind of clay called *pygg*. Over time, the clay jars were formed in the shape of a pig as a joke.

The Good Old Days

The cost of things such as movie tickets has changed a lot from when your grandparents were kids. In 1940, the average price of a movie ticket was about $.30. Today, the average movie ticket costs just under $8.00. Or you can buy the DVD of the movie and watch it many times for one low price.

Working from Home

Have you ever heard your parents say, "I wish I had another hour in the day to get everything done"? If you have, then you may have found an opportunity to make money. Think about what chores your parents usually do that you could help with. Could you set the table or clean up the kitchen after dinner? Maybe you could wash the family car every Saturday. Make a list of chores you know you can do and decide what payment you think is fair for each job. Sit down and talk with your parents about taking over a task or two from the list.

Plan Ahead

Scheduling your time makes it easier for you to get the job done and have time for other things like sports, homework, or just hanging out with friends. You can use a planner or cell phone app to keep track of your schedule.

A Little of Each

Some kids like to divide their time on the weekends between chores and fun. You might help with the laundry for the first part of the day. Then, you might spend the afternoon playing basketball with friends or reading your favorite book for fun. It feels great to help out and to have fun, too!

DIG DEEPER!

Pitching In

Why not build on the chores you already do? For example, if you wash the cars on Saturdays, offer to go the extra mile once a month. For extra money, you can wipe down the dashboards and vacuum. Going that extra step is a huge help. Your parents will appreciate it. And you could earn more money.

Bedroom

Make space for more cash. Sell old items or clothes to earn extra money.

Bathroom

Earn healthy rewards as you scrub away germs. How much would your parents pay to *not* have to clean the toilet?

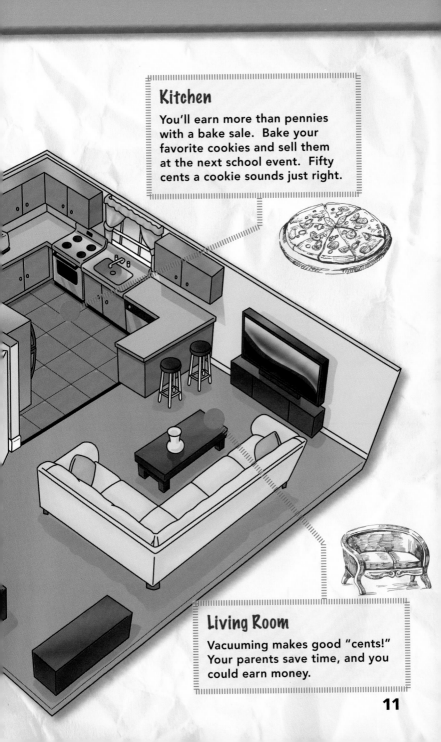

Kitchen

You'll earn more than pennies with a bake sale. Bake your favorite cookies and sell them at the next school event. Fifty cents a cookie sounds just right.

Living Room

Vacuuming makes good "cents!" Your parents save time, and you could earn money.

Becoming an Employee

When you work, someone pays you for what you do. When you are young, that someone may be your parents or a neighbor. When you work at a business, that person will be your **employer**. Take time now to develop the traits of a good **employee**. Most employers hire employees who are friendly, honest, punctual, and tidy. They also want someone who is willing to learn. Volunteer at your school, your church, or a local **charity**. Then, when you are old enough to get a job, you will already have many of the skills employers value.

Off to Work

In the United States, you can become an employee at 14 years old. In Europe, Australia, and New Zealand, you can't become a full-time employee until you're 14 or 15 years old. Businesses that employ children must follow special rules. Those rules say what type of work you can do and how many hours you can work each day.

Athletic teens may find work as lifeguards during the summer.

In the Money!

It's exciting to earn your own money—partly because there are so many ways to spend it! You might enjoy spending some money right away at a nearby arcade or a shopping center. Or maybe you want to see a new movie. You might plan to save for a more expensive item such as a bike or a new video game. Some kids like to save for unexpected costs in the future.

The First Impression

Have you ever heard the saying "You never get a second chance to make a first impression"? Studies show that it takes less than 10 seconds to make that first impression.

 Do

Smile.
Show you are a friendly person.

Dress in business attire.
Let people see that you respect the environment that you may one day work in.

Arrive early.
Let others know you are dependable.

Shake hands firmly and make eye contact.
Show the interviewer this meeting is important to you.

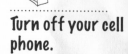

Turn off your cell phone.
Be clear that you value the time with your interviewer.

14

During an interview, the first 10 seconds are critical. You want the employer to like you and think you will be a good employee. Remember to make eye contact and smile. Dress up, speak with confidence, and shake hands. Read below to see what a difference a good first impression can make.

Don't

Answer your cell phone.

Interviewers will think you would rather be talking with your friends.

Arrive late.

This shows people you don't care if you get the job.

Give a limp handshake and look at the ground.

People will assume you aren't confident or up for the job.

Dress inappropriately.

Messy clothes make employers think you are not a team player or your style is more important than the company's image.

Stepping Stones

Your first job could be a step toward finding a career. Every job you have will give you new experiences that can help you learn and grow. Finding things you particularly like doing can give you hints about what careers you might like to pursue in the future. For instance, if you like babysitting, you might enjoy a career working with children. Consider whether you might want to be a teacher. Do you like walking the neighbor's dog? Maybe working with animals should be in your future. Consider becoming a veterinarian or an animal trainer. There are many jobs you can do now that will help you discover the type of work you will enjoy the most.

Growing Skills

Do you like babysitting?
Then try a career as a teacher or doctor.

Do you like dog walking?
Then try a career as a veterinarian.

Do you like mowing the lawn?
Then try a career as a landscaper.

Do you like cleaning the garage?
Then try a career as a professional organizer.

Jobs For All Seasons

Changes in weather offer new possibilities for chores around the house. Check out these ways to help out and make money as the seasons change.

Fall

Raking leaves can be a good way to earn money. Resist the urge to jump in them!

Winter

Shoveling snowy driveways and walkways can be hard work. Afterward, enjoy building a snowman or having a snowball fight.

Summer

After cutting the grass, a freshly mowed lawn would be a great place to play in the sprinklers on a hot summer day.

Spring

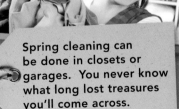

Spring cleaning can be done in closets or garages. You never know what long lost treasures you'll come across.

Building a Business

You don't have to wait to grow up to run your own business. Many kids manage their own small businesses. Some are even employers who oversee employees. If you have an idea for a business, you can become an **entrepreneur** (ahn-truh-pruh-NUR). An entrepreneur is someone with an idea who is willing to take a risk to make a **profit**. That means you think your idea is one that will make money.

teen skateboard shop owner Ian Youvan

Money Grower

Dustin Satloff loved baseball. He turned his passion for baseball into a business by designing bamboo baseball bats. First, he sold his bats to camp friends. Soon, his business grew. Satloff **patented** his bat design when he was 13. Why did he choose to make his bats out of bamboo instead of typical oak? Bamboo is stronger than oak and a better choice for the environment, too. Now that's a home-run idea!

Dustin Satloff

You're The Boss!

Entrepreneurs create new businesses. They work hard to organize and manage their companies. Most entrepreneurs are creative, motivated, and confident. They need to be able to think on their feet to handle unexpected problems, and they need to be willing to stay with a project when the going gets rough. Does that sound like you? As an entrepreneur, you will need to study your **target market**. These are the people who are most likely to buy your product or service. First, figure out what your market needs. Then, look for ways to create a product or service that fills that need. If you believe in your product or service, chances are that others will, too!

The Sky's the Limit

Lots of kids run lemonade stands. Other kids operate car-washing or pet-sitting businesses. Still others have newspaper routes, breed small animals, sell homegrown fruits and vegetables door to door, and more. There is no end to the ideas for businesses. Use your imagination. What do the people you know want or need that you can provide?

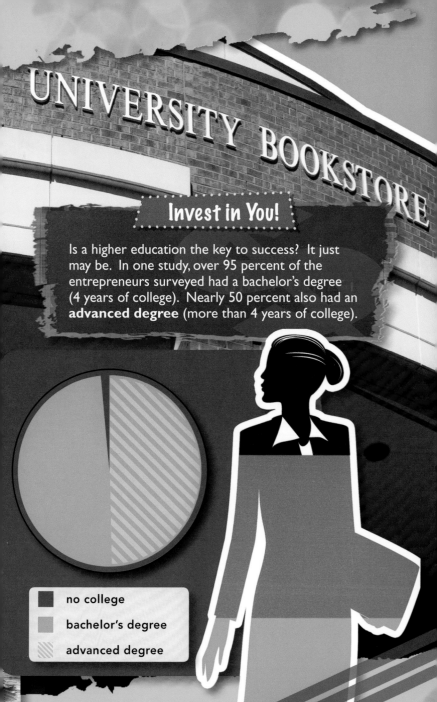

Invest in You!

Is a higher education the key to success? It just may be. In one study, over 95 percent of the entrepreneurs surveyed had a bachelor's degree (4 years of college). Nearly 50 percent also had an **advanced degree** (more than 4 years of college).

- no college
- bachelor's degree
- advanced degree

Do What You Love

What activities do you enjoy the most? Do you spend hours drawing or writing? Perhaps you could be an artist or a writer. Are you curious? Do you like to take things apart and reassemble them? **Engineering** might be a smart career for you. Or are you someone who enjoys working with others? Maybe running an after-school program is your dream. When deciding on which type of business to run, be sure that it taps into your personality and passion. People are usually better at doing things they enjoy. Doing what you love means you'll be having fun while working hard and making money.

Odd Jobs

Do you have an unusual hobby? Are you fascinated by weird stuff? There may be a job where you could put your special interests to work. People have made a living tasting ice cream, wrangling bees, making crossword puzzles, and test-driving new cars.

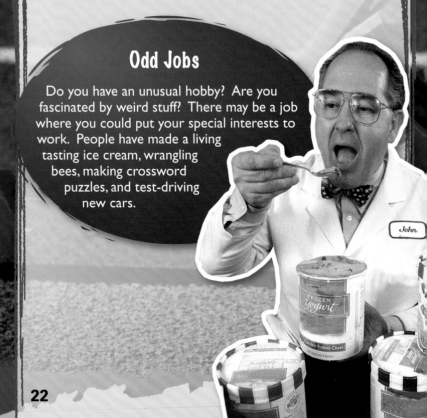

Practice Makes Perfect

If there is something you truly love doing, spend time learning how to do it well. The better you are at something like drawing or sports, the better chance you will have of making a living at it. So, practice, practice, practice! If you do, someday you may be among the lucky folks who do what they love and get paid for it!

Jamaican athlete Shelly-Ann Fraser-Pryce won one gold and two silver medals at the 2012 Summer Olympics in London. She competes in women's track and field sprinting events.

23

What Type of Entrepreneur Are You?

Working for yourself has its advantages. Many millionaires start out running their own businesses. What's the secret to their success? Finding a business that suits their passion and skills. Take this quiz to see what type of business could make you successful.

1 You've just received $20. You...

A. buy a movie, a book, or some music that inspires you.
B. buy a calculator or app that will simplify a school project.
C. call a friend and take her to the movies.

2 Your friend just lost the race for student council president. You...

A. make a card to cheer him up.
B. sit down and talk about strategies for another position.
C. gather all his supporters and organize a group hug.

3 You just signed up for the school bake sale. You volunteer to...

A. design an awesome email newsletter.
B. track all donations.
C. speak on stage and tell everyone about this great cause.

4 Your school has a Monday holiday. You...

A. spend the day gazing into the sky looking for shapes in the clouds.
B. get a jump on the school project that's due at the end of the week.
C. get your friends together and play softball.

If you scored mostly **As**, you are a Dreamer Entrepreneur. Your strengths are your imagination and the way you think "out of the box." You may prefer to work quietly alone while you develop your creative ideas. Next time you need advice on dreaming big, look to the successes of Dreamer Entrepreneur Steve Jobs for inspiration.

If you scored mostly **Bs**, you are a Problem-Solver Entrepreneur. Your strengths are critical thinking, planning, and organization. You approach problems as if they are fun puzzles to solve. You enjoy working alone and in a group. Study Problem-Solver Entrepreneur Bill Gates's work for tips and ideas.

If you scored mostly **Cs**, you are a People-Person Entrepreneur. Your strengths are caring for others and your ability to put yourself in somebody else's shoes. You tend to love working with others or for others. Check out People-Person Entrepreneur Oprah Winfrey's successes for ideas on how to make your next move.

Creating Your Business

Regardless of what type of business you run, it helps to organize a small home office. This is a special place set aside for you to do your work. You may just need a desk, a chair, and a lamp. Or you can stow a couple of boxes under your bed and pull them out when it is time to work. Does your family have a computer? Ask your parents if you can set up a folder on the computer. Save digital fliers, **invoices**, and any other business documents there for easy access.

Be Organized!

Successful business owners know where everything is when they need it. They keep their offices clean and free of clutter. A set of labeled folders will keep your invoices and **receipts** in order. A notebook will give you a place to write down your sales and **expenses**. A calendar will help you keep track of dates and deadlines.

Pull together a small supply of items such as paper, pencils, highlighters, paper clips, scissors, a stapler, and tape. Are you running a jewelry-making business? Then, you will need to buy the beads, wire, and tools to make your product. Are you selling items online? You'll need to have plenty of packing tape and boxes on hand to ship your items.

Don't Sell Yourself Short

One of the most essential skills for any business owner is figuring out how much to charge. It is important not to ask for too much, because that may drive **customers** away. But, it is just as important not to charge too little. So, how can you figure out what to charge? Calculate how long it will take you to make the product or provide the service, and factor that into your price. Then, check out what other people are charging for something similar. For instance, if you are a babysitter, investigate what other sitters are asking their **clients** to pay. Then, look at any extra or special conditions. Are you going to be responsible for caring for more than one child? Remember, three kids can be three times the work! That means you can and should charge more for your services.

When you sell a product, you set the amount you will charge. It's important to consider the cost of creating your product when you decide the price. Take a look at this example.

You will use an entire skein (SKEYN) of yarn to make a scarf. The skein costs $3.

+

$5 labor per hour
x 4 hours to knit
= $20

=

To make a profit, you should charge more than $23.

$23

29

The Bottom Line

To be successful, businesses need to make a profit. Profit is the difference between **revenue**, or sales, and the expenses involved in running a business. Business owners must look at all the costs involved. They must decide if there is enough money to buy materials, rent a space, or hire any additional employees. Then, they add up the money made from customers. They subtract the costs from the money earned. The money left is profit. Is this profit worth your time and energy? That's for you to decide!

Let's Do the Numbers

Imagine your summer business is running a game library. You add three games to your own home collection.

Expenses

Each game costs $10.
x 3 games
_____

That's a total of $30 to start your business.

Money Grower

Fifteen-year-old Pierce Freeman began studying computer programming when he was seven years old. As a teen, he spotted a **trend** in business. So, he made an app that would help make things simpler. He created CardShare to allow people to easily share their business contact information. He sold his app to Apple. Now, he is busy developing a new app to share with the market soon.

Revenue

Imagine you make $156 dollars over the summer.
$156 revenue
-$30 in expenses

That's $126 profit.

Was it worth it? If so, start planning for next summer. If not, dream up another moneymaking idea.

Sign on the Dotted Line

A **contract** is a written agreement between you and your client. A business contract lets you and your clients know exactly what they should expect to receive for their money. Contracts should include your company's name, the date of service, your name, the client's name and signature, details of the service, and how much you will be paid when the job is finished. Type up a contract like the one on the next page. Fill out one for each new project. Stamp it *paid* when the work is done and you have received payment.

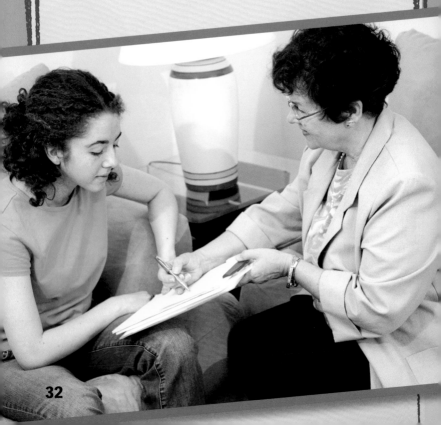

The Contents of a Contract

Whether you're a babysitter or a construction worker getting set to build a city bridge, a contract makes sure everyone knows their responsibilities. It tells **vendors** what services to provide. It tells clients when and how much to pay.

Pipsqueak Research Agency
12345 Consumer Drive
Revenue, NY 67891

Phone: 888-555-1234

Date: _____

Description of Service or Product:

_____

_____

Price charged for Service: _____

      # of hours to do the job _____ x _____ hourly rate

Price charged for Product: _____

      # of items customer is purchasing _____ x _____ the price of each item

Business Owner's Signature/Date: _____

Customer's Name (print): _____

Customer's Signature: _____

Date: _____

The Power of Planning

Entrepreneurs know the importance of a business plan. It's a step-by-step **strategy** for success. When you take time to plan up front, it's easier to imagine problems— and to find solutions. You may need to borrow money to start your company. A good business plan will convince lenders you are trustworthy and have a good idea. Here's what you'll need to get started.

Product or Service

Describe your product or service. Be clear on what you're selling.

BUSINESS PLA
SUMMER GAME LI

Product or service

The summer game library will be available for neighborhood kids over the course of the summer. The owner and operator of the game library will supervise and teach kids how to play new and old games. Games will include both indoor and outdoor games.

Finances

Finances

Note how much money will be needed to start the business. Describe how profitable the product will be.

STOP! THINK...

- What part of the business plan do you think is most important to lenders?

- What other information would be helpful to include in your plan?

- How do you think business plans help entrepreneurs be successful?

Marketing

List the ways you plan to tell people about your product.

game library will be advertise
throughout the neighborho
ool. Word of mouth and do
form parents and kids of th
rents and kids will learn tha
make summer better than

ment

er/manager
games and
ill be no ac
summer ga
ames piece
ies will be
er will asse

Management

Explain who will manage the business. Describe any special training you might have that makes you perfect for the job. Note if you will need any other employees.

Making Customers Happy

Customers are the people who purchase your products or services. They may be your friends or family. Or they might be people who hear about your business from others. It is important that your customers feel good about your work. People want to spend their money on excellent products. They want to know that when they pay you, the job will be done well. So listen to what your customers need before you start any job. And always do your best, whether the job is washing cars or dogs, babysitting hamsters or children, or cleaning pools or garages.

Bad News

One fourth of customers say they are more likely to share news of a bad business experience than of a good one. So keep your customers happy. Go the extra mile if you can. Customers will be your best advertisers!

Making It Right

Sometimes a customer isn't happy with your work. This can be hard to hear, but it's important to address the situation right away. Offer ways to fix it. Taking care of a customer means you are a responsible businessperson. Good news spreads fast. You may win new customers!

Happy customers spread good news.

Promoting Yourself

When you're selling a product or service, you're also selling yourself. Tell your family, friends, and neighbors about your business. Answer questions and be enthusiastic about your product. When you meet people, remember they might be potential clients. Mention your company. Explain why you started your business. When people believe you are capable and honest, they will trust the work you do.

Yes or No?

Studies show that most salespeople will receive at least five NOs before they get a YES. Don't get discouraged. With each NO, you are one step closer to a YES!

Asking for the Sale

Ask a successful salesperson what their sales secret is and many will say "I always ask for the sale." Studies show customers may be too shy to say, "I need that!" But if you ask for the sale, they just might give it to you.

I would be happy to sell you these apples. How can we seal the deal?

Promoting Your Product

You can sell yourself, but you'll also need to sell and **promote** your product. If you sell beaded bracelets, wear one every day, and show it off. If you plan to teach the neighborhood kids to play baseball, offer a free morning session. Design a flier to get the word out. Pass it out to friends and neighbors, and post it in public places. Take time to explain your product or service whenever you can. Ask your satisfied customers to spread the word about your business, too. **Word-of-mouth** is one of the most valuable marketing tools!

Clipping Coupons

Coupons are an easy way to get people excited about your product. Pass out coupons for a 10 percent discount or a small gift. These savings can get first-time customers excited enough to buy.

Saturday Night Babysitting
$10 per hour

10% OFF

Twelve-year-old Fabian Fernandez-Han invented the Oink-a-saurus app. This helpful app allows kids and adults to track their savings and investments right in the palms of their hands. What new handy app can you imagine and design?

Fernandez-Han attending a conference where he met with other entrepreneurs and traded ideas.

41

Designing a Flyer

A flyer is a great way to let people know about your product. Create something eye-catching. Keep it short and simple, but make sure you include all the key pieces of information.

Add pictures. Lay them out on the page so they look attractive.

List your contact information. Include your first name and phone number. Some people print this information several times in a row. Then, customers can easily tear off a copy.

World's (
Live

BABY APPROVED

Call Jamey a
555-739

Call Jamey
555-73

Call Ja
555-

Call Ja
55

Call
55

Write a short headline. Center it on one line across the page. Use type large enough that people can read it easily from 10 feet away. Capitalize the main words in the headline.

atest Babysitter

Your Block!

10 *per hour*

Available Friday and Saturday nights!

certified lifeguard
CPR Certified
lives with 5
ounger brothers

CALL JAMEY AT

5-7396

Include a description of your product or service. Keep it brief but be sure to use words that will interest future clients. Tell them what you are offering and why it's great.

Competitive Advantage

Get an edge on the competition by offering services that others don't. If most babysitters only work Wednesday nights, set yourself apart by working on weekends.

Eureka!

Inventions can be simple, like the paper clip. Or they can be complicated, like a new type of jet engine. Inventions can be helpful to people or give them new ways to have fun. They can also earn the inventor money.

A patent protects inventions. This legal document is filed with the government. It describes your invention and shows you are the inventor. If your invention is patented, no one else can claim they came up with your idea. And no one else can try to sell it.

Silly Bandz

In 2008, Silly Bandz hit the market, and their popularity spread fast. By 2010, Silly Bandz were sold in more than 8,000 stores throughout the United States. These wristbands are available in many colors and shapes. Kids wear them up and down their arms. Who will design the next **fad**? It could be you!

From Idea to Invention

1 Sketch your latest greatest idea.

2 Build a sample and test it to see if it works the way you expect.

3 Make changes to improve your product.

4 File a patent to protect your work.

PATENT APPLICATION

6 Sell your idea to the world. This is when the money starts flowing in.

5 Produce your product in larger numbers.

Growing Your Funds

You can make money by selling products or services. You can also make money, or grow your funds, in other ways. If you put your money in a **savings account**, the bank will pay you **interest** on it. Or you can put your money into a **certificate of deposit (CD)**. A CD grows at a faster rate than a savings account does. You can also put funds together with friends or neighbors and invest them in a local charity. Organize community events to collect money for a cause. Your money can be used to make the world a little bit better—for you, and for others.

Cashing in a CD

Investing in a CD is a reliable way to grow your money. But you won't be able to use your money for some time. It could be six months, five years, or longer. It's up to you. The longer your money stays in the account, the more it will grow.

Saving Money

One way to make your money grow is by finding ways to save it. Do you enjoy reading books or watching movies? You could buy books and go to the theater. Or you could head to your local library. There, you can check out items for free. Maybe you absolutely love the outfit on the cover of a new magazine. But you don't need to buy something new. Instead, you can update your favorite jeans and shirt with new **accessories** by adding hats, scarves, and jewelry. It will feel like a whole new outfit for a fraction of the cost.

Found Treasure

Historians believe pirates may have buried treasure off the coast of Florida. Can't get to Florida any time soon? Then start looking for buried treasure in your own home. Clean out your coat pockets. Look under the floor mats in the car. Take your coins to the local coin machine to turn those pennies into hard cash.

Ant or Grasshopper?

In Aesop's fable "The Ant and the Grasshopper," the ant works through the summer storing food. The grasshopper goofs off and plays music instead. When winter arrives, the grasshopper is hungry. He wishes he had planned ahead like the ant. Do you see yourself as a slow and steady ant-style saver? Or are you more of a got-to-have-it-now grasshopper?

Savings Accounts

How much money should you save? Many experts suggest that you set aside at least 10 percent of what you earn. When you open a savings account at a local bank, your savings will work for you by earning interest. Each month, the bank will pay you interest on the amount of savings you have in your account. The more money you have in your account, the more money you'll make.

The Power of 72

Money grows in a savings account, but how long will it take to double your money? Use the Power of 72. Simply divide 72 by the interest rate you will be receiving. Check out the example below.

You are getting 4 percent interest on your account.

72 ÷ 4 = 18

That means it will take 18 years to double your money.

Interest is paid on the original money placed in the account and on the interest earned each month. This is known as compound interest.

Interesting Interest

At 18 years old, you invest $2,000 in a CD. It has a 6 percent interest rate. Using the Power of 72, the chart below shows how your money will grow over time. Your money will double every 12 years. The best part is you never had to add another penny of your own money to that account.

18 years old	30 years old	42 years old	54 years old	66 years old
$2,000	$4,000	$8,000	$16,000	$32,000

Fund-raising

Do you have a favorite charity? One way to help is to raise money. As a **fund-raiser**, you will ask for donations and **pledges**. Donations can be made in the form of money, time, or recycled goods. Pledges are promises people make to contribute a certain amount of money. Do you like to walk or run? Find out if your favorite charity has a 5K run event. Join in and bring your family and friends. Your entrance fees will go to the charity and you can increase your donation by getting others to sponsor you with a pledge. If there is nothing planned for your area, think about hosting your own neighborhood run.

Kids Grow

Do you see problems in your community that you might help solve? Are there charities you would like to give to? Many opportunities are available. Ask your teacher or a community leader for ways you can help. Be sure to ask a parent before you begin a project.

Come Together

Fund-raisers use some of the same skills as entrepreneurs. You need to make a plan, solve problems, and get people excited to help. Entrepreneurs often work alone, but fund-raising is all about meeting new people. Working together is a fun way to raise money.

Good Business

The money skills you have can be used to help other people, too. You can use your business smarts to raise money for charity. Donate a percentage of your profits to your favorite group. Or try selling a new version of your product to raise awareness about a good cause. An inspirational bracelet is just one great way to spread the word.

Mt. Kilimanjaro

Money Grower

Jason Kontomitras set his sights high in the summer of 2010. He wanted to help blind and vision-impaired children in Guatemala. At 12 years old, he challenged himself to climb Mt. Kilimanjaro, one of the highest mountains in the world. He raised $26,000 in donations from supporters of his climb. Jason donated the money he raised to Vision for the Poor. This organization provides children with medical care to help them see.

Collecting even small amounts of money can make a big difference.

Families can walk together to support their favorite charities.

Good Money Grows

Eyes on the Prize

It's never too early to develop plans for your money. Creating good money habits now will help you succeed with your goals throughout your life. Keep your eyes on the prize by setting financial goals. Find ways to make yourself self-reliant. You'll grow your skills, confidence, and money! Just like a real tree, growing your money takes time and effort. But the more you know, the faster it will grow.

Why Not You?

Eighty-six percent of millionaires created their own fortunes. They didn't inherit their wealth. Many self-made millionaires are entrepreneurs. Through their ideas and hard work, they made it happen. Tell yourself, "If they can do it, so can I!"

> " Mighty things from small beginnings grow. "
>
> —John Dryden, English poet

Glossary

accessories—small objects or items of clothing carried or worn to add style to an outfit

advanced degree—a document that shows a person has completed higher levels of study

allowance—money given to a child so that he or she can learn about saving and spending money

certificate of deposit (CD)—a type of savings account that pays a fixed interest rate for a fixed amount of time

charity—an organization focused on helping others

chores—tasks done around the house

clients—customers

contract—a document that spells out the responsibilities of each person involved in a sale of goods or services

customers—people who purchase a product or service

employee—a person who works for someone else and is paid money

employer—a person who hires another to work for money

engineering—the science or profession of developing and using nature's power and resources in ways that are useful to people

entrepreneur—someone who runs his or her own business

expenses—money spent on products or services

fad—a product or idea that quickly becomes very popular for a short time

fund-raiser—a person or event who collects money to be donated to a charity or cause

interest—the money a bank or organization pays a person for investing in them

inventions—original ideas or objects that didn't exist before

invoices—itemized bills for goods sold or services provided, containing individual prices and the total charge due

labor—work done by a person for money

patented—acquired a legal document showing ownership of an invention

pledges—promises to pay an amount of money

profit—money earned after paying for the cost of producing a product or providing a service

promote—to help increase the sales of a product or service

receipts—written statements saying that money or goods have been received

revenue—money made from a sale

savings account—a type of bank account that pays the owner interest

self-reliant—independent and able to support oneself financially

strategy—a plan for achieving a specific goal

target market—a group of people who may want a certain product or service

trend—a current style or subject of interest

vendors—sellers

word-of-mouth—spoken communication

!ndex

Bibliography

Bateman, Katherine R. *The Young Investor: Projects and Activities for Making Your Money Grow, 2nd edition.* Chicago Review, 2010.

Learn about growing your money through stocks, mutual funds, and savings bonds. This book features fun projects that teach you how to balance a checking account, read the financial reports, understand mortgages, and more.

Bernstein, Daryl. *Better Than a Lemonade Stand!: Small Business Ideas for Kids.* Beyond Words Publishing, Incorporated, 2012.

Discover strategies for 51 different small businesses. This book includes details on the supplies and time needed to start a business as well as how much you should charge and how to advertise your services.

Linderman, Dianne. *How To Become An Entrepreneurial Kid.* The First Moms' Club Press, 2012.

Follow the stories of three inspiring entrepreneurial kids with cookie, fishing, and pony-ride businesses. Then, start your own business, using the planner at the end of the book.

Nathan, Amy. *The Kids' Allowance Book.* iUniverse, Incorporated, 2006.

Discover what over one hundred kids, their parents, and financial and psychology experts think about allowances. Topics include the pros and cons of an allowance, what to get paid, and how to make the most of your money.

Sember, Brette McWhorter. *The Everything Kids' Money Book.* Adams Media, 2008.

Learn everything you ever wanted to know about money! This book includes 30 puzzles and tons of cool facts to help you save, earn, and spend your money wisely.

More to Explore

Money and Stuff

http://www.moneyandstuff.info

Learn all about savings, budgets, credit, investing, and more. You'll also find worksheets to create your own budget, games, videos, and other fun activities.

Ten Inspirational Child Entrepreneurs

http://www.cosmoloan.com/investments/10-inspirational-child -entrepreneurs.html

Not sure you have what it takes to make your own money? Meet 10 young entrepreneurs. Their success in a range of industries— from online services and science card games to hair repair and pencil bugs—will inspire you to start your own business.

Kids' Money

http://www.kidsmoney.org/makemone.htm

Ready to make some money? Visit Kids' Money for ideas and tips on the right job for you. You might try babysitting, gardening, or one of the many other opportunities on this site. All of the suggestions for running your own business come from other kids just like you!

Money and Banking Videos

http://www.neok12.com/Banking.htm

These videos make money matters easy to understand. Learn about inflation, banking, how money is made, the history of the American dollar, and more.

Volunteer Opportunities for Kids

http://www.ivolunteer.org

Learn why and how kids across the country are getting involved in the community. Find links to volunteer organizations and projects just for kids.

About the Author

Kathleen E. Bradley's first memory about money took place when she was in the first grade. With five dollars in her pocket, she went shopping. She fell in love with a stuffed animal that cost $4.99. Kathleen got a penny in change. The cashier was surprised when Kathleen put down the toy and asked for her money back! With some convincing, she kept the toy. Yet decades later, she always weighs spending against the security that saving provides.

Kathleen E. Bradley is a contributor to the award-winning Teacher Created Materials *Building Fluency through Reader's Theater* for grades 1–5. She lives in Southern California with her husband and son.